Beyond Speed: Art and Evolution of Supercars and Hypercars

Etienne Psaila

Beyond Speed: The Art and Evolution of Supercars and Hypercars

Cover design by Etienne Psaila

Interior layout by Etienne Psaila

Foreword

As we stand at the forefront of automotive innovation, it is a privilege to present this comprehensive exploration of the world's most remarkable supercars and hypercars. This book is not just a collection of specifications and images; it is a tribute to the relentless pursuit of excellence in automotive engineering and design.

In these pages, you will encounter machines that represent the zenith of human ingenuity and creativity in the automotive field. Each car is a convergence of art and science, a harmonious blend of aesthetics, power, and cutting-edge technology. From the roar of a V12 engine to the whisper-quiet efficiency of electric motors, this book captures the diverse spectrum of advancements that define the modern automotive era.

These cars are more than mere vehicles; they are the embodiment of dreams and the pinnacle of aspiration. They reflect the unwavering dedication of designers, engineers, and visionaries who push the boundaries of what is possible. In every curve, in every line, and in every technical innovation, there lies a story of challenges overcome, limits pushed, and benchmarks set.

This book invites you to journey into the heart of automotive passion, to explore the marvels of engineering that have set the world's racetracks and roads alight. It is a celebration of speed, power, and beauty, a testament to the human spirit's endless quest for progress and perfection.

As you turn these pages, may you be inspired by the boundless creativity and unyielding determination that these vehicles represent. May you glimpse the future through the lens of the present, and may you appreciate the incredible journey of automotive evolution that has brought us to this point.

Welcome to a world where dreams meet reality, where innovation knows no bounds, and where the road ahead is an open canvas of possibilities. Welcome to the extraordinary world of supercars and hypercars.

Bugatti Chiron

1. Technical Specifications:

- **Engine Type:** 8.0-liter quad-turbocharged W16

- **Displacement:** 7,993 cc

- **Horsepower:** 1,479 hp at 6,700 rpm

- **Torque:** 1,600 Nm at 2,000-6,000 rpm

- **Transmission Type:** 7-speed dual-clutch automatic

- **Drive Type:** All-wheel drive

- **0-60 mph Acceleration Time:** 2.5 seconds

- **Top Speed:** Electronically limited to 261 mph (420 km/h)

- **Braking System:** Carbon ceramic brakes with 8-piston calipers at the front and 6-piston at the rear

- **Suspension:** Independent suspension with a complex system for variable ride height and firmness

2. Design and Aerodynamics:

- **Exterior Styling:** Sleek and flowing lines with the iconic Bugatti horseshoe grille. A mix of carbon fiber and aluminum panels.

- **Aerodynamic Features:** Adaptive rear wing/spoiler, strategically placed air intakes, and diffusers for optimal downforce and cooling.

- **Interior Design:** Luxurious and bespoke, with leather, carbon fiber, and aluminum finishes. Digital instrumentation and classic analog speedometer.

- **Seating Capacity:** Two-seater.

3. Technology and Features:

- **Infotainment System:** High-end sound system, infotainment with navigation and telemetry data.

- **Connectivity Features:** Bluetooth, hands-free calling, and an integrated media interface.

- **Advanced Driver Assistance Systems (ADAS):** Limited due to focus on driving experience, but includes parking sensors and rear-view camera.

- **Unique Technological Innovations:** Launch control, sophisticated stability control system, and a mode selector for different driving dynamics.

4. Performance Metrics:

- **Track Performance:** Renowned for its stability and speed on tracks, though not primarily designed as a track-focused hypercar.

- **Handling Characteristics:** Remarkable stability and handling at high speeds, aided by advanced aerodynamics and all-wheel-drive system.

- **Fuel Efficiency:** Around 5.4 miles per gallon city and 14.7 mpg highway (though not a primary concern for its owners).

The Bugatti Chiron stands as a marvel of modern automotive engineering, blending incredible performance with luxurious design. It's a perfect example of what a hypercar can achieve in terms of speed, design, and technological innovation.

Koenigsegg Jesko

1. Technical Specifications:

- **Engine Type:** 5.0-liter twin-turbocharged V8

- **Displacement:** 5,000 cc

- **Horsepower:** Up to 1,578 hp on E85 biofuel (1,280 hp on regular gasoline)

- **Torque:** 1,500 Nm

- **Transmission Type:** 9-speed Light Speed Transmission (LST) with multiple clutches

- **Drive Type:** Rear-wheel drive

- **0-60 mph Acceleration Time:** Approx. 2.5 seconds

- **Top Speed:** Claimed to exceed 300 mph (483 km/h)

- **Braking System:** Carbon ceramic brakes with 6-piston calipers

- **Suspension:** Triplex suspension at rear, double wishbones with adaptive dampers

2. Design and Aerodynamics:

- **Exterior Styling:** Aggressive and aerodynamic with Koenigsegg's signature dihedral synchro-helix door mechanism.

- **Aerodynamic Features:** Active rear wing, front splitter, and large diffusers for maximum downforce.

- **Interior Design:** Minimalist yet luxurious, with exposed carbon fiber, leather, and Alcantara.

- **Seating Capacity:** Two-seater.

3. Technology and Features:

- **Infotainment System:** Koenigsegg's proprietary system with full connectivity.

- **Connectivity Features:** Bluetooth, Wi-Fi, and a comprehensive telematics system.

- **Advanced Driver Assistance Systems (ADAS):** Includes essentials like traction control, but limited due to the car's performance focus.

- **Unique Technological Innovations:** Autoskin (robotized body openings), advanced active chassis with adaptive ride height.

4. Performance Metrics:

- **Track Performance:** Built for exceptional track performance with a focus on agility and speed.

- **Handling Characteristics:** Extremely responsive, designed to handle high speeds with stability.

- **Fuel Efficiency:** Not a primary focus for this vehicle category.

McLaren P1

1. Technical Specifications:

- **Engine Type:** 3.8-liter twin-turbocharged V8 with an electric motor

- **Displacement:** 3,799 cc

- **Horsepower:** Combined 903 hp (727 hp from the V8 and 176 hp from the electric motor)

- **Torque:** 900 Nm combined

- **Transmission Type:** 7-speed dual-clutch automatic

- **Drive Type:** Rear-wheel drive

- **0-60 mph Acceleration Time:** Approximately 2.8 seconds

- **Top Speed:** Electronically limited to 217 mph (350 km/h)

- **Braking System:** Carbon-ceramic brakes with regenerative braking capabilities

- **Suspension:** Hydro-pneumatic suspension with variable ride height and damping

2. Design and Aerodynamics:

- **Exterior Styling:** Futuristic design with dihedral doors and extensive use of carbon fiber.

- **Aerodynamic Features:** Active aerodynamics with an adjustable rear wing and underbody flaps to optimize downforce and drag.

- **Interior Design:** Minimalist and driver-focused, with carbon fiber elements and a digital instrument cluster.

- **Seating Capacity:** Two-seater.

3. Technology and Features:

- **Infotainment System:** Focused on driving with limited infotainment features to save weight.

- **Connectivity Features:** Basic connectivity options.

- **Advanced Driver Assistance Systems (ADAS):** Limited to essentials, focus on driving purity.

- **Unique Technological Innovations:** Hybrid powertrain, Instant Power Assist System (IPAS) for on-demand electric power.

4. Performance Metrics:

- **Track Performance:** Known for exceptional track capabilities, agile and responsive handling.

- **Handling Characteristics:** Precise steering and exceptional grip.

- **Fuel Efficiency:** Enhanced by the hybrid system, offering better efficiency than traditional supercars.

McLaren Speedtail

1. Technical Specifications:

- **Engine Type:** 4.0-liter twin-turbocharged V8 with hybrid system

- **Displacement:** 4,000 cc

- **Horsepower:** Combined output of 1,055 hp

- **Torque:** 1,150 Nm

- **Transmission Type:** 7-speed dual-clutch automatic

- **Drive Type:** Rear-wheel drive

- **0-60 mph Acceleration Time:** Approx. 2.9 seconds

- **Top Speed:** 250 mph (403 km/h)

- **Braking System:** Carbon ceramic brakes, designed for high-performance and durability

- **Suspension:** Active suspension system, designed for both comfort and performance

2. Design and Aerodynamics:

- **Exterior Styling:** Streamlined, teardrop-shaped bodywork for maximum aerodynamic efficiency

- **Aerodynamic Features:** Unique aerodynamic design with integrated rear ailerons, front-wheel static aero covers, and a flat underbody

- **Interior Design:** Luxurious, futuristic design with a unique central driving position flanked by two passenger seats

- **Seating Capacity:** Three-seater, with the driver's seat positioned centrally

3. Technology and Features:

- **Infotainment System:** State-of-the-art infotainment system with touchscreens for both driver and passengers

- **Connectivity Features:** Advanced connectivity options including Bluetooth and integrated interfaces

- **Advanced Driver Assistance Systems (ADAS):** Features include parking sensors and cameras, with minimal intrusion to maintain the driving experience

- **Unique Technological Innovations:** Electrostatically dimmable glass, retractable digital rear-view cameras in place of traditional mirrors, bespoke personalization options

4. Performance Metrics:

- **Track Performance:** Optimized for high-speed efficiency rather than traditional track performance

- **Handling Characteristics:** Exceptional high-speed stability and smooth handling, with a focus on straight-line performance

- **Fuel Efficiency:** Hybrid system enhances efficiency, but exact figures are secondary to performance

The McLaren Speedtail represents a blend of luxury, innovation, and extreme performance, epitomizing the cutting-edge technology and design ethos of McLaren. It's a hypercar designed not just for speed, but also as a statement of technological achievement and exclusive craftsmanship.

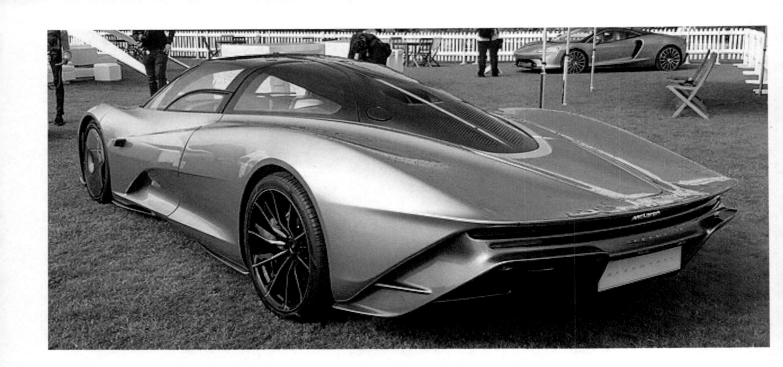

LaFerrari

LaFerrari - Technical Specifications, Design, Aerodynamics, Technology, and Features

1. Technical Specifications:

- **Engine Type:** 6.3-liter naturally aspirated V12 with HY-KERS hybrid system

- **Displacement:** 6,262 cc

- **Horsepower:** Combined output of 950 hp (800 hp from the V12 engine and 150 hp from the electric motor)

- **Torque:** Over 900 Nm

- **Transmission Type:** 7-speed dual-clutch automatic

- **Drive Type:** Rear-wheel drive

- **0-60 mph Acceleration Time:** Less than 3 seconds

- **Top Speed:** Over 217 mph (350 km/h)

- **Braking System:** Brembo carbon-ceramic brakes with regenerative braking system

- **Suspension:** Active magnetorheological damping system

2. Design and Aerodynamics:

- **Exterior Styling:** Designed for aerodynamic efficiency, featuring Ferrari's signature design language with modern and aggressive lines

- **Aerodynamic Features:** Active aerodynamics with movable front diffusers and a rear spoiler, along with a smooth underbody

- **Interior Design:** Driver-focused cockpit with minimalistic design, carbon fiber elements, and digital displays

- **Seating Capacity:** Two-seater

3. Technology and Features:

- **Infotainment System:** Minimalist approach to infotainment to keep focus on driving experience

- **Connectivity Features:** Basic connectivity features, emphasizing driving rather than connectivity

- **Advanced Driver Assistance Systems (ADAS):** Limited to essential features to maintain focus on the driving experience
- **Unique Technological Innovations:** HY-KERS hybrid system for enhanced performance and efficiency, F1-derived KERS technology for energy recovery

4. Performance Metrics:

- **Track Performance:** Exceptional track performance with a focus on handling and speed, benefiting from hybrid powertrain
- **Handling Characteristics:** Precise and responsive handling, aided by advanced aerodynamics and the car's hybrid architecture
- **Fuel Efficiency:** While more efficient than traditional V12 engines due to the hybrid system, fuel efficiency is not the primary focus

LaFerrari is not just a symbol of Ferrari's engineering prowess, but also a milestone in the automotive world. It blends state-of-the-art technology, breathtaking performance, and the soulful character of a Ferrari. This hypercar represents a harmonious fusion of extreme power with environmental consciousness, thanks to its innovative hybrid system. It's a testament to Ferrari's commitment to pushing the boundaries of what's possible in a high-performance car, marrying tradition with innovation. LaFerrari stands as a pinnacle achievement, not only for the brand but for the entire realm of automotive engineering, embodying a perfect balance between advanced technology and the passionate spirit of Italian supercar craftsmanship.

Bugatti Centodieci

1. Technical Specifications:

- **Engine Type:** 8.0-liter quad-turbocharged W16

- **Displacement:** 7,993 cc

- **Horsepower:** 1,600 hp

- **Torque:** 1,600 Nm

- **Transmission Type:** 7-speed dual-clutch automatic

- **Drive Type:** All-wheel drive

- **0-60 mph Acceleration Time:** 2.4 seconds

- **Top Speed:** Electronically limited to 236 mph (380 km/h)

- **Braking System:** High-performance carbon ceramic brakes

- **Suspension:** Sophisticated suspension setup for optimal handling and comfort

2. Design and Aerodynamics:

- **Exterior Styling:** Inspired by the EB110, it features modern reinterpretation of its classic lines, combined with Bugatti's signature design elements

- **Aerodynamic Features:** Optimized for downforce and cooling, with strategically placed air intakes, vents, and a fixed rear wing

- **Interior Design:** Luxurious and customizable, featuring the finest materials such as leather, carbon fiber, and aluminum

- **Seating Capacity:** Two-seater

3. Technology and Features:

- **Infotainment System:** Advanced system with navigation, multimedia, and telemetry features

- **Connectivity Features:** Standard connectivity options including Bluetooth

- **Advanced Driver Assistance Systems (ADAS):** Includes essential safety features, but with a focus on driving purity

- **Unique Technological Innovations:** Advanced aerodynamics, lightweight construction techniques, and unique W16 engine configuration

4. Performance Metrics:

- **Track Performance:** While not solely track-focused, it delivers exceptional performance and handling on the track

- **Handling Characteristics:** Precise and agile, with a focus on high-speed stability and cornering

- **Fuel Efficiency:** As with most hypercars, fuel efficiency is not a primary concern, but it's consistent with high-performance vehicles of its caliber

The Bugatti Centodieci stands as a remarkable homage to the brand's rich history, while simultaneously showcasing its prowess in modern hypercar design and technology. This hypercar is not just a tribute to the past but a statement of Bugatti's commitment to innovation and exceptional performance, making it a truly extraordinary machine in the world of automotive engineering.

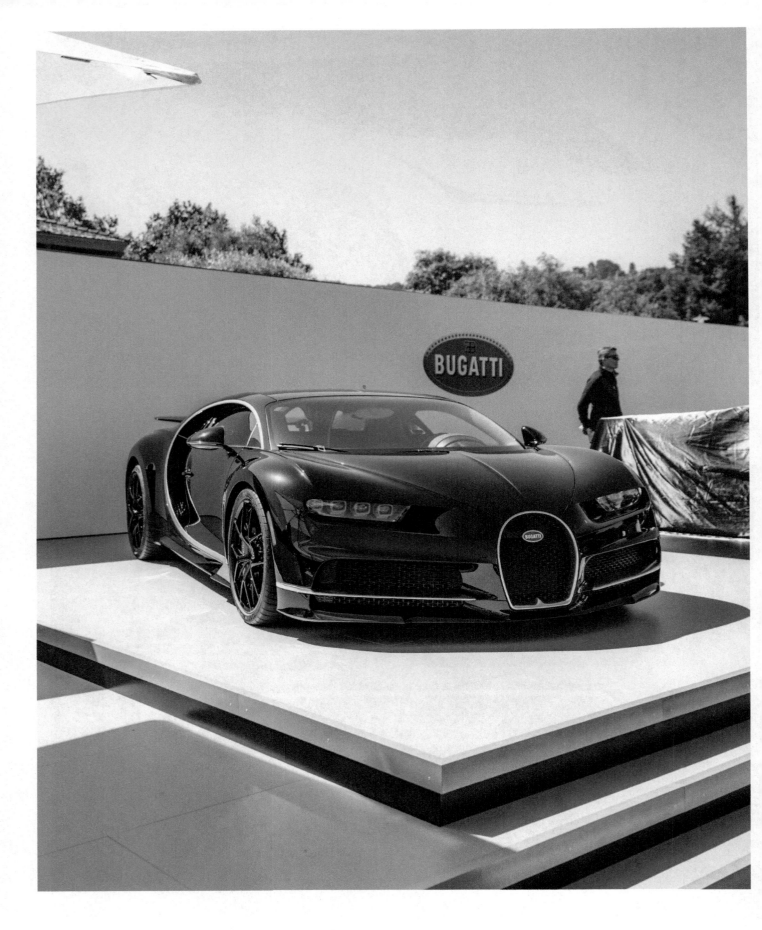

Porsche 918 Spyder

1. Technical Specifications:

- **Engine Type:** 4.6-liter naturally aspirated V8 with two electric motors

- **Displacement:** 4,593 cc

- **Horsepower:** Combined output of 887 hp (608 hp from the V8 engine and 279 hp from electric motors)

- **Torque:** Over 1,280 Nm combined

- **Transmission Type:** 7-speed PDK dual-clutch automatic

- **Drive Type:** All-wheel drive (with electric motors powering the front wheels)

- **0-60 mph Acceleration Time:** 2.6 seconds

- **Top Speed:** 214 mph (345 km/h)

- **Braking System:** High-performance carbon ceramic brakes

- **Suspension:** Adaptive suspension system with multiple modes

2. Design and Aerodynamics:

- **Exterior Styling:** Futuristic and aerodynamic design with Porsche's distinctive styling cues

- **Aerodynamic Features:** Active aerodynamics with adjustable rear wing, diffuser, and underbody panels for optimized downforce

- **Interior Design:** Driver-focused cockpit with a blend of luxury, sportiness, and advanced technology

- **Seating Capacity:** Two-seater

3. Technology and Features:

- **Infotainment System:** Advanced Porsche Communication Management system with navigation, media, and connectivity options

- **Connectivity Features:** Bluetooth, USB, and other standard Porsche connectivity options

- **Advanced Driver Assistance Systems (ADAS):** Includes Porsche's typical range of safety and assistance features

- **Unique Technological Innovations:** Hybrid drive system with plug-in capability, regenerative braking, and multiple driving modes for different performance levels

4. Performance Metrics:

- **Track Performance:** Exceptional track capability, balanced with the flexibility of hybrid technology for road use

- **Handling Characteristics:** Precision handling typical of Porsche, enhanced by the low center of gravity and hybrid system's torque vectoring.

- **Fuel Efficiency:** The 918 Spyder offers better fuel efficiency compared to conventional supercars, thanks to its hybrid system. It can even run on electric power alone for short distances, emitting zero emissions in this mode.

The Porsche 918 Spyder is a remarkable blend of cutting-edge technology, sustainable performance, and traditional Porsche driving dynamics. It represents a significant step in the evolution of sports cars, showcasing how hybrid technology can enhance rather than compromise the driving experience. With its innovative features, the 918 Spyder has set new standards for hypercars, especially in terms of integrating electric power with traditional high-performance engines. Its legacy is not just in its speed or technology, but in its demonstration that environmental consciousness and supreme performance can coexist in the world of supercars.

918 Spyder

Ford GT

1. Technical Specifications:

- **Engine Type:** 3.5-liter EcoBoost V6 twin-turbocharged
- **Displacement:** 3,497 cc
- **Horsepower:** 647 hp
- **Torque:** 550 lb-ft (746 Nm)
- **Transmission Type:** 7-speed dual-clutch automatic
- **Drive Type:** Rear-wheel drive
- **0-60 mph Acceleration Time:** Approximately 3.0 seconds
- **Top Speed:** 216 mph (348 km/h)
- **Braking System:** Brembo carbon-ceramic brakes
- **Suspension:** Pushrod suspension, adjustable ride height

2. Design and Aerodynamics:

- **Exterior Styling:** Futuristic yet reminiscent of the classic GT40, with aerodynamic and sleek lines
- **Aerodynamic Features:** Active rear wing, extensive underbody aerodynamics including diffusers, and vented wheel arches
- **Interior Design:** Minimalist and driver-focused, with digital instrumentation and carbon fiber elements
- **Seating Capacity:** Two-seater

3. Technology and Features:

- **Infotainment System:** Sync 3 infotainment system with touchscreen, including navigation and connectivity features
- **Connectivity Features:** Bluetooth, USB ports, and smartphone integration
- **Advanced Driver Assistance Systems (ADAS):** Basic ADAS features focusing on performance driving, including rear-view camera
- **Unique Technological Innovations:** Lightweight carbon fiber construction, active aerodynamics, and EcoBoost engine technology for performance and efficiency

4. Performance Metrics:

- **Track Performance:** Designed with a focus on track performance, offering exceptional handling and speed

- **Handling Characteristics:** Razor-sharp handling with an emphasis on stability and grip, benefiting from advanced aerodynamics and chassis design

- **Fuel Efficiency:** Decent for a supercar, but as with most vehicles in its class, not a primary concern

The Ford GT stands as a testament to Ford's rich racing heritage and its ability to innovate in the realm of high-performance automobiles. This supercar not only pays homage to the legendary GT40 with its striking design but also pushes the boundaries of modern technology and engineering. It's a vehicle that beautifully balances raw power with sophisticated aerodynamics and lightweight construction, making it a formidable presence on both the road and the racetrack. The Ford GT is more than just a fast car; it's a symbol of American ingenuity and a benchmark in the world of supercars, reflecting Ford's commitment to excellence in performance and design.

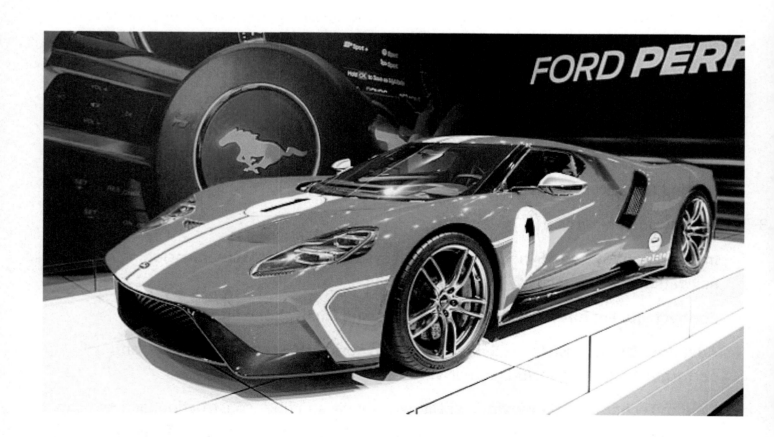

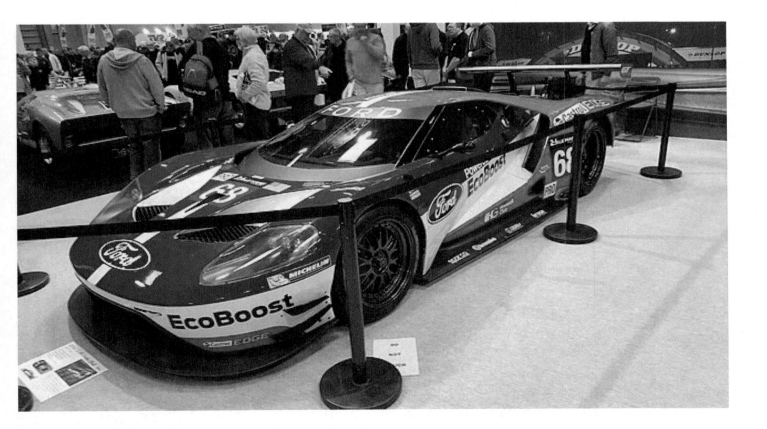

Aston Martin Valkyrie

1. Technical Specifications:

- **Engine Type:** 6.5-liter naturally aspirated V12 with hybrid system

- **Displacement:** 6,498 cc

- **Horsepower:** Combined output of around 1,160 hp (1,014 hp from the V12 engine and 160 hp from the electric motor)

- **Torque:** 900 Nm

- **Transmission Type:** 7-speed Ricardo dual-clutch automatic

- **Drive Type:** Rear-wheel drive

- **0-60 mph Acceleration Time:** Estimated under 2.5 seconds

- **Top Speed:** Estimated over 250 mph (402 km/h)

- **Braking System:** Brembo carbon-ceramic brakes

- **Suspension:** Pushrod-operated inboard springs and dampers

2. Design and Aerodynamics:

- **Exterior Styling:** Futuristic and highly aerodynamic design, with extensive use of carbon fiber and radical aerodynamic elements

- **Aerodynamic Features:** Ground-effect aerodynamics with a massive rear diffuser, active aero elements, and a venturi tunnel design

- **Interior Design:** Extremely minimalist and driver-focused, with a "feet-up" Formula 1-style seating position

- **Seating Capacity:** Two-seater

3. Technology and Features:

- **Infotainment System:** Stripped down to essentials for weight saving; focuses more on performance data than entertainment

- **Connectivity Features:** Basic connectivity, with emphasis on driving and performance data

- **Advanced Driver Assistance Systems (ADAS):** Limited, as the focus is on pure driving experience

- **Unique Technological Innovations:** High-performance hybrid powertrain, advanced lightweight construction, and unique aerodynamic design

4. Performance Metrics:

- **Track Performance:** Engineered primarily for track performance with extraordinary handling and speed capabilities

- **Handling Characteristics:** Exceptional handling with F1-inspired technology, offering a driving experience akin to a race car

- **Fuel Efficiency:** Not a primary consideration, with the focus being on maximizing performance

The Aston Martin Valkyrie represents a bold step into the future of hypercars, merging track-level performance with road car versatility. It's an engineering marvel that showcases the pinnacle of Aston Martin's design and technological capabilities, setting new benchmarks for what a hypercar can achieve. The Valkyrie is more than just a vehicle; it's an expression of extreme performance, innovation, and an uncompromising pursuit of automotive perfection.

Rimac Nevera

1. Technical Specifications:

- **Engine Type:** Four electric motors (one for each wheel)

- **Total Power Output:** 1,914 hp

- **Torque:** 2,360 Nm

- **Transmission Type:** Single-speed transmission for each motor

- **Drive Type:** All-wheel drive with torque vectoring

- **0-60 mph Acceleration Time:** 1.85 seconds

- **Top Speed:** 258 mph (412 km/h)

- **Battery Capacity:** 120 kWh lithium-manganese-nickel battery

- **Range:** Up to 340 miles (547 km) on a single charge (WLTP cycle)

2. Design and Aerodynamics:

- **Exterior Styling:** Sleek, futuristic design with a focus on aerodynamic efficiency

- **Aerodynamic Features:** Active aerodynamics including an adjustable rear wing, diffuser, and underbody flaps

- **Interior Design:** High-tech and luxurious, with digital displays and customizable interfaces

- **Seating Capacity:** Two-seater

3. Technology and Features:

- **Infotainment System:** State-of-the-art infotainment system with multiple touchscreens and advanced connectivity

- **Connectivity Features:** Wi-Fi, Bluetooth, and comprehensive smartphone integration

- **Advanced Driver Assistance Systems (ADAS):** Includes advanced safety features and driver assistance technologies

- **Unique Technological Innovations:** Cutting-edge electric powertrain, advanced cooling systems, regenerative braking system

4. Performance Metrics:

- **Track Performance:** Exceptional performance with instant torque delivery and sophisticated torque vectoring for superior handling

- **Handling Characteristics:** Precise and agile handling, benefiting from the low center of gravity and advanced chassis dynamics

- **Energy Efficiency:** Highly efficient electric powertrain, with regenerative braking to maximize range

The Rimac Nevera is a showcase of what's possible in the realm of electric hypercars. It's not just an incredibly fast car; it represents a paradigm shift in automotive engineering, proving that electric vehicles can deliver exhilarating performance that rivals, and in some aspects surpasses, traditional internal combustion engine supercars. The Nevera stands as a testament to Rimac's vision and expertise in electric vehicle technology, marking a significant milestone in the evolution of the hypercar.

Lamborghini Sián FKP 37

1. Technical Specifications:

- **Engine Type:** 6.5-liter V12 with a 48-volt mild-hybrid system

- **Displacement:** 6,498 cc

- **Horsepower:** Combined output of 819 hp (785 hp from the V12 engine and 34 hp from the electric motor)

- **Torque:** 720 Nm

- **Transmission Type:** 7-speed ISR (Independent Shifting Rod) automatic

- **Drive Type:** All-wheel drive

- **0-60 mph Acceleration Time:** Less than 2.8 seconds

- **Top Speed:** Over 217 mph (350 km/h)

- **Braking System:** High-performance carbon-ceramic brakes

- **Suspension:** Pushrod suspension system with active dampers

2. Design and Aerodynamics:

- **Exterior Styling:** Aggressive and futuristic, featuring Lamborghini's iconic sharp lines and hexagonal design elements

- **Aerodynamic Features:** Active aerodynamic system with an adjustable rear wing and innovative cooling system through its unique design

- **Interior Design:** Luxurious and driver-centric, with advanced digital displays and customizable options

- **Seating Capacity:** Two-seater

3. Technology and Features:

- **Infotainment System:** Lamborghini's advanced infotainment system with a fully digital driver's display

- **Connectivity Features:** Standard connectivity options including Bluetooth and Lamborghini's infotainment interface

- **Advanced Driver Assistance Systems (ADAS):** Includes essential features for safety and convenience, but focused on a purist driving experience

- **Unique Technological Innovations:** First use of a supercapacitor in a hybrid setup, offering three times the power of a battery of the same weight

4. Performance Metrics:

- **Track Performance:** Designed for both road and track use, offering exceptional performance and handling

- **Handling Characteristics:** Sharp and responsive handling, typical of Lamborghini's supercars, enhanced by the hybrid system

- **Fuel Efficiency:** Improved efficiency due to the hybrid system, although performance remains the primary focus

The Lamborghini Sián FKP 37 is a bold step into the future of supercars for the iconic brand. It seamlessly blends Lamborghini's legendary V12 engine with innovative hybrid technology, symbolizing a bridge to a new era while maintaining the unmistakable Lamborghini DNA. The Sián is not just a showcase of raw power and cutting-edge design, but also a testament to Lamborghini's commitment to pioneering new technologies in the realm of high-performance vehicles.

Ferrari SF90 Stradale

1. Technical Specifications:

- **Engine Type:** 4.0-liter twin-turbocharged V8 with three electric motors

- **Displacement:** 3,990 cc

- **Horsepower:** Combined output of 986 hp (769 hp from the V8 engine and 217 hp from electric motors)

- **Torque:** 800 Nm

- **Transmission Type:** 8-speed dual-clutch automatic

- **Drive Type:** All-wheel drive (with electric motors powering the front wheels)

- **0-60 mph Acceleration Time:** 2.5 seconds

- **Top Speed:** 211 mph (340 km/h)

- **Braking System:** High-performance carbon-ceramic brakes

- **Suspension:** Adaptive magnetic ride suspension

2. Design and Aerodynamics:

- **Exterior Styling:** Modern and aggressive design, maintaining Ferrari's distinctive styling elements

- **Aerodynamic Features:** Active aerodynamics with a shut-off Gurney, front underbody vortex generators, and a rear spoiler

- **Interior Design:** Driver-oriented cockpit with a mix of luxury and functionality, featuring digital displays and minimalistic controls

- **Seating Capacity:** Two-seater

3. Technology and Features:

- **Infotainment System:** State-of-the-art Ferrari infotainment system with a large central touchscreen and digital driver display

- **Connectivity Features:** Bluetooth, smartphone integration, and advanced navigation systems

- **Advanced Driver Assistance Systems (ADAS):** Includes Ferrari's suite of driver assistance technologies

- **Unique Technological Innovations:** Plug-in hybrid system, eManettino for electric drive mode selection, and advanced torque vectoring

4. Performance Metrics:

- **Track Performance:** Exceptional performance capabilities, designed to excel both on the road and the track

- **Handling Characteristics:** Precise and responsive handling, benefitting from the hybrid powertrain and advanced aerodynamics

- **Fuel Efficiency:** Improved efficiency for a supercar due to the hybrid system, with the ability to drive on electric power alone for short distances

The Ferrari SF90 Stradale represents a significant milestone in Ferrari's history, marking their foray into electrified performance vehicles. It combines the raw emotion and power of a traditional Ferrari supercar with the innovation and efficiency of modern hybrid technology. The SF90 Stradale is a testament to Ferrari's commitment to pushing the boundaries of automotive performance and design, setting a new standard in the world of luxury sports cars.

FERRARI 75 YEARS

Pagani Huayra

1. Technical Specifications:

- **Engine Type:** 6.0-liter twin-turbocharged V12 (sourced from Mercedes-AMG)

- **Displacement:** 5,980 cc

- **Horsepower:** 730 hp

- **Torque:** 1,000 Nm

- **Transmission Type:** 7-speed single-clutch automated manual

- **Drive Type:** Rear-wheel drive

- **0-60 mph Acceleration Time:** About 2.8 seconds

- **Top Speed:** 238 mph (383 km/h)

- **Braking System:** Brembo carbon-ceramic brakes

- **Suspension:** Independent double wishbone with adjustable coilovers

2. Design and Aerodynamics:

- **Exterior Styling:** Exquisite and artistic, featuring a blend of modern and classic design elements, extensive use of carbon fiber and unique gull-wing doors

- **Aerodynamic Features:** Active aerodynamics with four movable flaps to adjust downforce dynamically

- **Interior Design:** Luxurious and bespoke, with a combination of leather, carbon fiber, and aluminum; every detail customizable

- **Seating Capacity:** Two-seater

3. Technology and Features:

- **Infotainment System:** Customizable according to the buyer's preferences, typically includes a touchscreen with navigation and sound system

- **Connectivity Features:** Basic connectivity options with an emphasis on the driving experience over digital features

- **Advanced Driver Assistance Systems (ADAS):** Limited; the focus is more on driving engagement

- **Unique Technological Innovations:** Carbotitanium monocoque chassis for lightweight strength, active aerodynamics for stability and efficiency

4. Performance Metrics:

- **Track Performance:** While not solely a track-focused car, it offers exceptional performance and handling on both track and road

- **Handling Characteristics:** Razor-sharp and responsive, with a focus on driver feedback and engagement

- **Fuel Efficiency:** As a hypercar, its focus is on performance rather than fuel efficiency

The Pagani Huayra is a masterpiece of automotive engineering and design, blending artistic craftsmanship with cutting-edge technology. It's not just a hypercar in terms of speed and performance; it's also a testament to Horacio Pagani's vision of creating a moving work of art. The Huayra stands out for its attention to detail, bespoke customization, and its unique position as a bridge between modern technology and traditional craftsmanship in the world of supercars.

Mercedes-AMG One

1. Technical Specifications:

- **Engine Type:** 1.6-liter turbocharged V6 with four electric motors

- **Displacement:** 1,600 cc

- **Horsepower:** Combined output of over 1,000 hp

- **Torque:** Not officially disclosed, but expected to be substantial given its hybrid powertrain

- **Transmission Type:** 8-speed automated manual

- **Drive Type:** All-wheel drive (with electric motors powering the front wheels)

- **0-60 mph Acceleration Time:** Estimated under 2.7 seconds

- **Top Speed:** 217 mph (350 km/h)

- **Braking System:** High-performance carbon-ceramic brakes

- **Suspension:** Active suspension system, adjustable for varying conditions

2. Design and Aerodynamics:

- **Exterior Styling:** Aggressive and futuristic design, heavily influenced by Formula 1 technology and aesthetics

- **Aerodynamic Features:** Active aerodynamic components including a deployable rear wing, front flaps, and venturi tunnels

- **Interior Design:** Focused and minimalist, with a digital cockpit and F1-style steering wheel, prioritizing functionality over luxury

- **Seating Capacity:** Two-seater

3. Technology and Features:

- **Infotainment System:** Simplified system focusing on driving data and essential information, rather than entertainment

- **Connectivity Features:** Basic connectivity with an emphasis on performance telemetry and vehicle dynamics

- **Advanced Driver Assistance Systems (ADAS):** Limited to essential safety features to maintain the focus on driving performance

- **Unique Technological Innovations:** Formula 1-derived hybrid powertrain, sophisticated energy recovery system, and track-focused dynamics

4. Performance Metrics:

- **Track Performance:** Engineered with a focus on track prowess, offering exceptional handling, acceleration, and top speed

- **Handling Characteristics:** Extremely sharp and responsive, benefiting from F1 technology and a lightweight structure

- **Fuel Efficiency:** While more efficient than conventional supercars due to its hybrid system, performance remains the primary focus

The Mercedes-AMG One is a true embodiment of Formula 1 technology applied to a road car. It's a vehicle that blurs the line between a hypercar and a Grand Prix racer, bringing unparalleled performance and engineering excellence to the road. This car is not just a statement of Mercedes-AMG's capabilities in high-performance automotive engineering, but it's also a showcase of how hybrid technology can be applied to achieve extreme speed and agility, marking a significant moment in the evolution of supercars.

Lotus Evija

1. Technical Specifications:

- **Engine Type:** Four electric motors

- **Total Power Output:** 2,000 hp

- **Torque:** 1,700 Nm

- **Transmission Type:** Single-speed automatic

- **Drive Type:** All-wheel drive with torque vectoring

- **0-60 mph Acceleration Time:** Under 3 seconds

- **Top Speed:** Over 200 mph (322 km/h)

- **Battery Capacity:** 70 kWh

- **Range:** Approximately 250 miles (402 km) per charge

2. Design and Aerodynamics:

- **Exterior Styling:** Strikingly futuristic design, featuring a dramatic aerodynamic shape and dihedral doors

- **Aerodynamic Features:** Active aerodynamics with an integrated air diffuser and an innovative Venturi tunnel design for exceptional downforce

- **Interior Design:** Minimalist and driver-focused, with advanced digital displays and luxurious materials

- **Seating Capacity:** Two-seater

3. Technology and Features:

- **Infotainment System:** Advanced system tailored for driver engagement and vehicle monitoring

- **Connectivity Features:** Modern connectivity options with an emphasis on performance data

- **Advanced Driver Assistance Systems (ADAS):** Focus on driving purity, with essential safety features

- **Unique Technological Innovations:** One of the most powerful all-electric hypercars, with advanced battery technology and ultra-fast charging capabilities

4. Performance Metrics:

- **Track Performance:** Designed for exceptional performance on both road and track, with a focus on handling and acceleration

- **Handling Characteristics:** Agile and responsive, benefiting from the low center of gravity and sophisticated chassis technology

- **Energy Efficiency:** High energy efficiency with rapid charging capabilities, setting a new standard in electric hypercar performance

The Lotus Evija marks a significant step in the evolution of hypercars, being one of the most powerful all-electric hypercars ever conceived. It combines Lotus's renowned handling and lightweight ethos with groundbreaking electric powertrain technology, showcasing a new era of performance and efficiency in the automotive world. The Evija is not only a statement of Lotus's capabilities in high-performance vehicle engineering but also a glimpse into the future of electric mobility in the supercar segment.

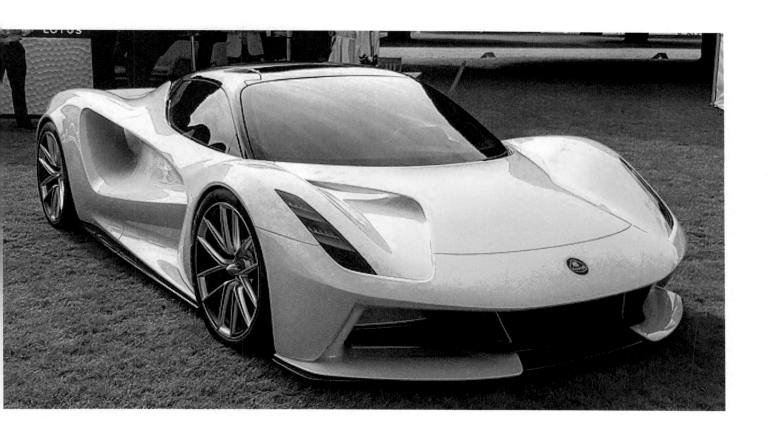

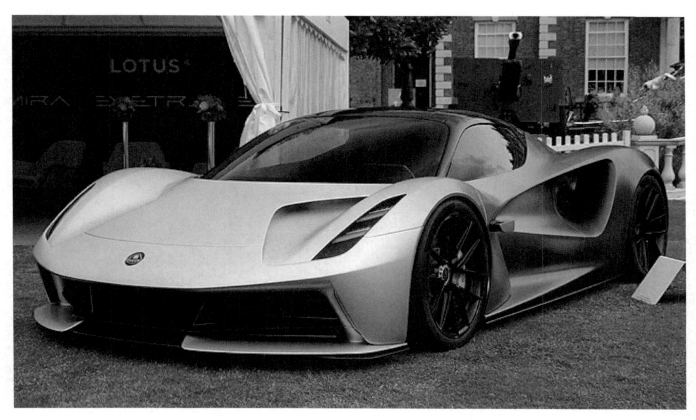

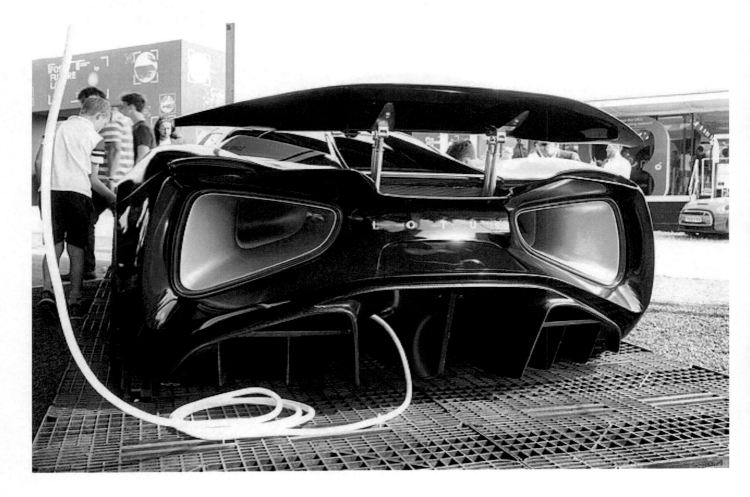

NIO EP9

1. Technical Specifications:

- **Engine Type:** Four electric motors (one at each wheel)

- **Total Power Output:** 1,341 hp (1 megawatt)

- **Torque:** 1,480 Nm

- **Transmission Type:** Individual gearboxes for each motor

- **Drive Type:** All-wheel drive with torque vectoring

- **0-60 mph Acceleration Time:** 2.7 seconds

- **Top Speed:** 217 mph (350 km/h)

- **Battery Capacity:** 777V lithium-ion battery pack

- **Range:** Approximate range of 265 miles (427 km) under the New European Driving Cycle (NEDC)

2. Design and Aerodynamics:

- **Exterior Styling:** Sleek, futuristic design with a focus on aerodynamic efficiency

- **Aerodynamic Features:** Active aerodynamic system including an adjustable rear wing and a flat floor design for optimal downforce and stability

- **Interior Design:** Minimalist and race-focused, with digital displays and essential controls

- **Seating Capacity:** Two-seater

3. Technology and Features:

- **Infotainment System:** Focused on driving data and performance metrics, less on conventional infotainment

- **Connectivity Features:** Basic connectivity focused on vehicle and performance data

- **Advanced Driver Assistance Systems (ADAS):** Limited to essentials, prioritizing performance and driving experience

- **Unique Technological Innovations:** One of the fastest electric hypercars, advanced regenerative braking system, and interchangeable battery system

4. Performance Metrics:

- **Track Performance:** Exceptional track capabilities with record-setting lap times at various circuits

- **Handling Characteristics:** Precise and responsive, benefitting from the advanced torque vectoring system

- **Energy Efficiency:** High efficiency with fast charging capabilities, representing the forefront of electric vehicle technology

The NIO EP9 is a testament to China's growing prowess in the electric vehicle sector, specifically in the high-performance and luxury segments. It showcases cutting-edge technology, impressive performance capabilities, and a vision for the future of electric hypercars. The EP9 is not just a symbol of NIO's commitment to innovation but also a strong contender in the global arena of electric supercars, demonstrating the potential of electric powertrains to compete with and even surpass traditional combustion-engine supercars in terms of performance and technological advancement.

McLaren Senna

1. Technical Specifications:

- **Engine Type:** 4.0-liter twin-turbocharged V8

- **Displacement:** 3,994 cc

- **Horsepower:** 789 hp

- **Torque:** 800 Nm

- **Transmission Type:** 7-speed dual-clutch automatic

- **Drive Type:** Rear-wheel drive

- **0-60 mph Acceleration Time:** 2.8 seconds

- **Top Speed:** 208 mph (335 km/h)

- **Braking System:** Carbon ceramic discs with McLaren's bespoke brake calipers

- **Suspension:** RaceActive Chassis Control II (RCC II) with adaptive dampers

2. Design and Aerodynamics:

- **Exterior Styling:** Extremely aggressive and functional, designed purely for aerodynamic efficiency and downforce

- **Aerodynamic Features:** Active aerodynamics with a prominent rear wing, front splitter, and diffuser; extensive use of carbon fiber for weight reduction

- **Interior Design:** Spartan and track-focused, with exposed carbon fiber, minimalistic controls, and a focus on driver engagement

- **Seating Capacity:** Two-seater

3. Technology and Features:

- **Infotainment System:** McLaren's infotainment system with a focus on performance data, minimalistic to save weight

- **Connectivity Features:** Essential connectivity features, with a focus on lightweight and performance

- **Advanced Driver Assistance Systems (ADAS):** Limited to essential features to reduce weight and maintain focus on driving purity

- **Unique Technological Innovations:** Extensive use of carbon fiber for chassis and body, active aerodynamics, and a focus on track performance

4. Performance Metrics:

- **Track Performance:** Engineered primarily for track use, offering exceptional handling, braking, and cornering capabilities

- **Handling Characteristics:** Razor-sharp and highly responsive, with a chassis tuned for maximum driver feedback and engagement

- **Fuel Efficiency:** As a track-focused hypercar, fuel efficiency is not a primary concern

The McLaren Senna is a tribute to the legendary Formula 1 driver Ayrton Senna, reflecting his focus on pure driving ability and performance. It's a hypercar that prioritizes track performance above all else, combining McLaren's latest technology, engineering prowess, and a relentless pursuit of speed and agility. The Senna represents the pinnacle of McLaren's design and engineering capabilities, offering an unparalleled driving experience that's as close as possible to a race car while still being road legal.

SSC Tuatara

1. Technical Specifications:

- **Engine Type:** 5.9-liter twin-turbocharged V8

- **Displacement:** 5,900 cc

- **Horsepower:** 1,750 hp on E85 fuel (1,350 hp on 91 octane gasoline)

- **Torque:** 1,735 Nm

- **Transmission Type:** 7-speed automated manual

- **Drive Type:** Rear-wheel drive

- **0-60 mph Acceleration Time:** Approximately 2.5 seconds

- **Top Speed:** Claimed to be over 300 mph (483 km/h)

2. Design and Aerodynamics:

- **Exterior Styling:** Futuristic and sleek design with a focus on aerodynamic efficiency and high-speed stability

- **Aerodynamic Features:** Designed for minimal drag and optimal downforce, featuring active aerodynamics

- **Interior Design:** Driver-centric with a focus on performance, combining luxury and functionality

- **Seating Capacity:** Two-seater

3. Technology and Features:

- **Infotainment System:** Advanced system designed for both performance monitoring and entertainment

- **Connectivity Features:** Standard modern connectivity options, tailored for a hypercar experience

- **Advanced Driver Assistance Systems (ADAS):** Basic features, focusing on driver engagement and vehicle control

- **Unique Technological Innovations:** Advanced carbon fiber construction for lightweight and strength, active aerodynamics for high-speed stability

4. Performance Metrics:

- **Track Performance:** Exceptional track capabilities, particularly in terms of top speed and acceleration

- **Handling Characteristics:** Precise and responsive handling, engineered for both high-speed stability and agility on the track

- **Fuel Efficiency:** While not a primary focus for hypercars, it offers efficiency improvements over traditional supercars due to its advanced engineering

The SSC Tuatara is a remarkable example of American engineering and design in the hypercar segment. It represents SSC North America's ambition to compete with the fastest cars in the world, showcasing not only extreme speed but also advanced aerodynamics and engineering. The Tuatara is a testament to the company's commitment to pushing the boundaries of performance and technology, aiming to set new standards in the hypercar market.

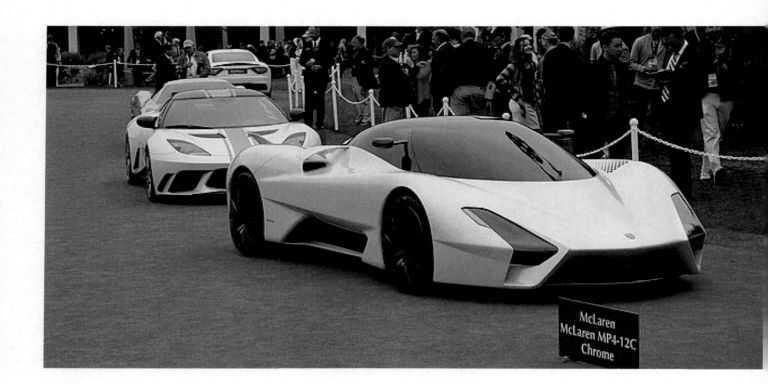

Conclusion

In conclusion, this book represents a journey through the pinnacle of automotive engineering and design, showcasing some of the most extraordinary supercars and hypercars the world has ever seen. From the groundbreaking electric innovation of the Rimac Nevera to the unparalleled speed of the SSC Tuatara, each car in this collection stands as a testament to human ingenuity, passion, and the relentless pursuit of perfection.

Through detailed specifications, vivid photography, and insightful narratives, we have explored the unique character and groundbreaking technologies of each model. These cars are not just means of transportation; they are works of art, symbols of technological advancement, and embodiments of the dreams and aspirations of their creators.

As we close this book, we recognize that these vehicles are more than just the sum of their parts. They are the result of decades of automotive evolution, a fusion of science and artistry, and a showcase of what becomes possible when boundaries are pushed and conventions challenged. They remind us that the pursuit of excellence is a never-ending journey and that the future of automotive design and technology is limited only by our imagination.

Let this book serve not just as a record of what has been achieved but also as an inspiration for what is yet to come. The world of supercars and hypercars is ever-evolving, and with each passing year, new marvels will emerge, pushing the limits of speed, design, and innovation even further. As we turn the final page, we look forward with anticipation to the next chapter in this thrilling story of automotive excellence.

About the Author

Etienne Psaila: An Accomplished Author and Educator

With a writing journey spanning two decades, Etienne Psaila has long been passionate about crafting stories. For many years, he wrote purely for the pleasure it brought, sharing his works exclusively with a close circle of friends and family. It was only recently, spurred by the enthusiastic feedback from his readers, that he ventured into the realm of publishing. Today, his works are available in various formats, from eBooks to paperbacks.

Etienne holds a Bachelor of Education degree from the prestigious University of Malta. For the past 20 years, he has devoted himself to the noble profession of teaching. His commitment to education is evident not only in the classroom but also in the written word, as he occasionally authors short stories tailored for his students. He firmly believes that his teaching experiences enrich his storytelling, offering a unique perspective that sets his work apart.

Diverse in his literary pursuits, Etienne delves into various genres, ranging from historical and romantic fiction to thrillers and science fiction. Recognizing the ever-evolving reading habits in our fast-paced world, he also pens concise narratives, perfect for a two or three-sitting read. These shorter tales serve as an ideal alternative for those who might not have the time to immerse themselves in lengthier novels and for those seeking a break from the constant influx of social media. Whether long or short, fiction or non-fiction, Etienne's books cater to a wide audience.

Currently, Etienne calls the beautiful island nation of Malta home.

Image Credits:

All images in this book were taken by me, are public domain or used under the Creative Commons Attribution 2.0 and 4.0

- Tony Patt
- Ank gsx
- Mr. Walkr
- el.guy08_11
- Robert Rouse
- Caleryn88
- Liam Walker
- Alexandr Migl
- Y.Leclercq
- Axion23
- Rutger van der Maar
- Michelin LIVE UK
- Sarah Larson
- Paulius Malinovskis
- Maxim Pierre
- Ford Chip Ganassi Team UK
- Kieran White
- Greg Gjerdingen
- Dave Doe
- Adam Court
- Vauxford
- Mr. choppers
- Ank Kumar
- pelican-actor
- Rutger van der Maar
- Clemens Vasters
- Autoviva
- Matti Blume
- Andrew Basterfield
- NearEMPTiness
- Chelsea Jay
- Jengtingchen
- Phil Guest
- Tristan Surtel
- J.Smith831

Printed in Great Britain
by Amazon

35054237R00057